# THE 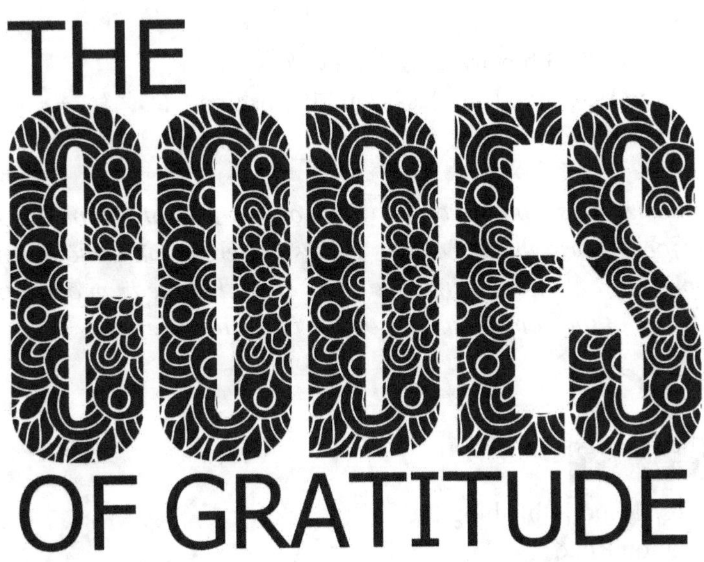 CODES

## OF GRATITUDE

GREGORY JASZEWSKI

Proofreading: Joanna Sosnowka
Text correction: Anna Gajowniczek
Text composition: InkWander
Cover design: InkWander

ISBN: 9788396928177

Limitless Mind Publishing Ltd
15 Carleton Road
Chichester
PO19 3NX
England
Tel. +44 7747761146
Email: office@limitlessmindpublishing.com

*Dear Reader!*

*Find us on **Facebook/Instagram**:*
*limitless mind publishing*

*And visit our page on **Amazon***
*by entering: limitless mind publishing into the search bar or by scanning the QR code to see our other titles.*

**♥*We would greatly appreciate your opinion about the book*. *It means a lot to us.***

*Dedication*

*With a smile on my face and a tear of joy, I want to express in words the depth of my gratitude for everything you are and everything you have brought, bring, and will bring into my world and spaces.*

*Your love, friendship, and support have been, are, and will continue to be a constant source of energy and light in my life, and your smile warms my heart with joy.*

*Your energy encourages me to reach my highest potential and explore new levels of creativity. Your help is always invaluable, and our shared moments are a book of countless adventures.*

*Most importantly, your hearts show me a love that I will never forget.*

*Thank you for being who you are - strong, courageous, kind, compassionate, beautiful souls that bring so much beauty and joy into my spaces.*

*Your presence is inspiring, and I thank you for being a guiding light in my journey through the corners of everyday life.*

*With endless admiration and appreciation, to the wonderful beings and energies, and all their forms and manifestations contained within the creation and the word "woman".*

*Gregory*

# INVITATION

On the crossroads of day and night, heaven and earth, stands a tree that serves as a bridge between the beginning and infinity, possessing the power to awaken true potential.

It is the gateway to The Codes of Gratitude, where it is said that, with the right intentions, anything is possible. Amidst the rustling leaves and towering branches of this majestic tree, an elusive path winds its way, capable of transporting you to other dimensions.

According to an unknown legend, by partaking in fasting and contemplation at the foot of this sacred tree, one can uncover their true purpose and awaken their power.

It is a journey through time, meant to outline the story of your life and inspire you to shape your future with utmost grace and luxury. May The Codes of Gratitude guide you towards your dreams, for surely beneath their weathered bark lies a world of abundance, waiting for those ready to discover it.

I invite you to embark on this journey!

# DISCLAIMER

I have written this compilation solely for informational purposes, but I have made every effort to make it comprehensive and as accurate as possible. Therefore, this book should be used as a guide rather than the ultimate source. The purpose of this compilation is for educational purposes. The author and publisher do not guarantee that the information contained herein is fully complete, and furthermore, they do not accept responsibility for any errors or omissions. The author and publisher disclaim any liability towards any individual or entity for any loss or damage caused or allegedly caused directly or indirectly by this book.

# FOR WHOM? WHY? WHAT FOR?

**Who can benefit from and who are the Codes of Gratitude aimed at:**

**Individuals diagnosed** with or experiencing emotional and nervous imbalances, depression, loneliness, exclusion, and lack of self-acceptance and acceptance of their environment.
**Development coaches** who want to help clients experience the many benefits of Gratitude.
**Authors writing** about self-improvement, as they can utilize the knowledge in the book to deepen their awareness of improving well-being through acknowledgment.
**Health and well-being bloggers,** as this compilation will expand the range of topics for discussion with diverse content that will interest readers.
**Speakers and trainers** who can draw insights and examples from this content to illustrate improved well-being through Gratitude.
**Counselors and therapists** who can work with their patients to explain the challenges caused by a lack of Gratitude and offer positive solutions that impact their patients' lives.
**Individuals desiring to awaken joy,** happiness, and health in their lives.

**How can the Codes of Gratitude help you?**

• You will create a reward for positive changes in your life.
• You will discover creative ways to express Gratitude to loved ones.
• You will practice strengthening the value of your life through Grati-

tude.
• You will learn how to feel Gratitude in difficult situations.
• You will elevate your mood through Gratitude-building strategies.
• You will take the time to reflect on what you have and begin to nurture it.
• You will gain a better understanding of the benefits of Gratitude and how they can make your life more fulfilling.

# INTRO

William Arthur Ward once said,

"Gratitude can transform common days into thanksgivings, turn routine jobs into joy, and ordinary opportunities into blessings."

**What does Gratitude mean?**

Gratitude is a quality, a mental attitude of being fully thankful for all the gifts that come with being present here and now, as well as being ready to appreciate and help others. It is awakening the ability to notice and contemplate all the things we have been blessed with and the people who surround us. Gratitude is one of the fundamental keys to a happy and abundant life. When you express gratitude for what you have, you are content with your life and all the positives it has to offer. Regardless of circumstances, there is always something to be grateful for. In fact, studies conducted by Robert A. Emmons and Michael E. McCullough have shown that experiencing positives enhances brain chemistry and provides powerful energy for both health and relationships (1). Therefore, it is worth programming positives within ourselves and our lives. They serve as a powerful lever in moments of choice or doubt.

If we are able to be grateful for everything we have, we open the doors to even greater fortune, wonderful people, and promising opportunities, allowing us to see more of them on our path.

"Wanderer, there is no path. The path is made by walking..." Antonio Machado.

If you feel a lack of gratitude in your life and fear that it may be emptiness, it is time to take action and learn how you can develop gratitude to experience a happier life. If you are currently facing a difficult life situation and believe that you cannot be grateful, it is time to learn how to cultivate gratitude and reach a higher level. With determination and effort, you can quickly develop a sense of gratitude and become a person who is content with yourself and your life.

You can immerse yourself in the mysteries of gratitude and explore the benefits it can bring to your life. If you are ready to improve your overall well-being and live a happier life, learn to develop gratitude and reach a higher level.

Gratitude, like any skill, can be learned and cultivated as a habit. If you want to increase the impact of positives on your own life, nurturing a mindset of gratitude is a great way to do so.

# CHAPTER 1

## Gratitude Definition

Almost every day, we say thank you. Unconsciously, we mention it at the grocery store checkout and in our local café, but are these sincere expressions of gratitude or just learned responses?

**What exactly is gratitude?**

Is it something different than saying "thank you," or is thanksgiving itself an element of gratitude?

Focus and discover, while listening or maybe reading the Codes of Gratitude, how simple "thank-yous" can have a powerful impact on both the giver and the recipient. This is particularly a natural process when the words reflect genuine feelings of gratitude. So, the question arises, what exactly is gratitude?

The Roman philosopher Cicero described gratitude as the greatest of virtues and the parent of all others. It is the key that opens all doors and is a quality that makes us and keeps us youthful.

This statement made over two thousand years ago is fascinating. It speaks of gratitude as a virtue or a quality of existence. Gratitude is precisely such a power. Gratitude is also an emotion. It is something we deeply feel in our hearts. We can feel it towards others when people are grateful to us or when we witness someone expressing gratitude to another. Being grateful in the interactions or exchanges between people comes naturally. Yet, in trying to understand this simplicity, we may find more complex meanings in the words spoken to us or by us. Gratitude is an emotion, an experience, and can be a deliberate choice of consciousness. Connections in our relationships are both strengthened and supported by the power of gratitude.

In its essence, gratitude holds the experience of universal belonging. We can experience it as a general sense of well-being when we practice intentional cultivation of gratitude in our lives and begin to discover and experience its true value.

## Gratitude as a state of being

Take a moment, close your eyes, and try to remember a moment or event in your life when you felt appreciated, valued. Awaken it and think about it as if it were happening right now. Use the questions I prepared and add your own suggestions and experience that state.

What words did you hear?
What did your body feel like at that moment?
What caused that experience?
What were you thinking at that moment?
What do you enjoy most about being appreciated?
What about that particular moment made you remember it until today?

Write down your answers to these questions in the Chronicle of the Land of Gratitude, which you can refer to later.

There is no single definition of gratitude. Gratitude has been conceptualized and defined in the context of attitudes, emotions, morality, traits, habits, and even coping strategies in difficult situations. Gratitude is undoubtedly an incredibly complex and dynamic emotion. It is an ability that contributes to satisfaction in interpersonal relationships.

## Gratitude as an emotion

In this context, we must ensure that we distinguish emotions from moods. An emotion pertains to something or someone. It relates to a personal significant circumstance or experience. On the other hand, a mood is not tied to any object and is not dependent on a single factor. By exploring gratitude in this way, we see that it occurs in response to actions within relationships. Something is given by someone and received by someone else. This exchange helps strengthen feelings of gratitude.

Gratitude is an empathetic emotion, which means that to experience the emotion, the recipient must be in the position of the giver. Feeling grateful in response to a gift requires the recipient to sense the giver's positive intention. It is this recognition and empathetic connection that form the basis of the emotional experience of gratitude in the interaction.

We can express gratitude for many reasons. We can be grateful for personal benefits, such as advice from a mentor, or we can be grateful for material objects, such as a gift, our home, or our car. Gratitude can also be supported through interpersonal fulfillment, such as a hug from a friend. We can experience gratitude for financial benefits, such as a raise at work, and even for small coins tossed to us by angels that are worth noticing on our path through everyday life.

# CHAPTER 2

# Finding gratitude in society

When we look at the United States today, many see a wealthy, admired, and powerful nation. It is not respected solely for its military might and technological advancements, but for the freedoms enjoyed by its citizens, enabling them to pursue their dreams.

The founding values of the nation served as a model for all who came after the bloody war for independence. The United States and what it is today were shaped by waves of immigrants who embraced higher values, setting the country on a path of progress. While the early years were challenging for them, they learned to adapt and survive harsh winters, overcoming weaknesses and expanding their comfort zone.

Realizing that hard work was the only way to change their current situation and achieve success in their new lives, they learned to express gratitude for the opportunities they received in each moment.

It was gratitude for the simple gifts that every second brought into their lives, for having a roof over their heads and food on the table. This allowed them to grow and ride the wave of small yet significant accomplishments forward.

As those who came before us have proven, gratitude can play a significant role in shaping our destiny, creating our here and now.

## Gratitude in Today's World

In highly consumeristic society, where quarterly growth has become a measure of national standing, possessing a killer instinct is seen as a great asset, raising the question of whether there is still room for gratitude.

We can hypothesize that we all strive for happiness, but our ways of finding it vary. Some try to attain it through service and love, while others seek it in esoteric books or at the feet of gurus. Unfortunately, the majority of us attempt to find happiness through the acquisition of material goods. This has transformed society into one that feels entitled to everything it receives and achieves, rejecting the idea of expressing gratitude for what it has. Many of us view things through the lens of sales and purchases, and some even apply this framework to relationships with people. This means that they see others from the perspective of using and discarding them based on their needs.

And here comes the surprise that may catch you off guard. Gratitude is as contagious as materialism. Once you realize that gratitude can help you achieve what you desire, you simply begin to practice it and experience it.

# CHAPTER 3

# Application of gratitude in relationships

Falling into the feverish routine of daily life, it's easy to forget to express our appreciation to those who are most important to us. Take a moment to reflect on the relationships in your life, pinpointing the person/people, personalizing the time and circumstances when you felt gratitude. One of the most common mistakes we can make in our relationships is assuming that the other person will behave according to our expectations. This happens when we assume that someone in our life knows what we think or feel. The problem is that if we don't let the people in our lives who are important to us know that they matter to us, we won't initiate the thread of gratitude towards them.

Most of us have stopped consciously existing in our lives. We've turned on autopilot and simply drift through life. Our brains and bodies have become so familiar with our routine that we don't pay much attention to our everyday lives. Our minds are usually busy making lists, reminding us of daily events, or thinking ahead—we've lost mindfulness. We tend to bypass the experienced emotions that we know so fluidly, missing out on all the nuances of the experience in the process.

**Expressing Gratitude Developing**

A greater awareness of gratitude can have an impact on the cause-and-effect relationships of our existence. There is evidence that by sharing our gratitude, whether through kindness, words, or gifts, we nurture our relationships, helping them grow stronger. Knowing that this makes sense, we need to explore how we can convey our appreciation to those who are most important to us.

While there's nothing wrong with expressing gratitude by saying "thank you" or "great job," these expressions of gratitude are often taken for granted and rarely convey the strong and valuable message we would like them to convey. One way you can express your appreciation that promotes connection in relationships is by incorporating three elements into your expression:

- observation,
- feeling,
- need.

By sharing your observation, you simply state what you observe. It's like holding the door open, doing the dishes, or taking out the trash. These everyday actions take on a different dimension, but we often fail to recognize that. Sometimes just letting someone know that you noticed something can make that person feel deeply appreciated. Then, you need to let that person know that what they did has had a positive impact on you.

The final aspect of expressing gratitude is often the most challenging moment. It can be difficult for us to accept that we need others, but we must do so. It's important to remember that we don't exist in small bubbles and that we are constantly influenced by those around us. Telling someone that they matter when you need them is an open door to connect with others.

When it comes to relationships, don't limit your expression of gratitude to when people give you things or do something for you. Sometimes, sharing gratitude for who they are as individuals is equally valuable. Let the people in your life know that you appreciate not only what they do for you but also who they are to you. It's worth praising someone's generosity, kindness, and compassion, but the greatest value lies in simply acknowledging and recognizing who these individuals are to us. See for yourself how this works in your own backyard.

# CHAPTER 4

## V e power of positive emotions and gratitude

The desire to be happy is a realistic aspiration; however, it seems that we are misinformed about what happiness truly is. Sometimes, we may think that we have found happiness in a new computer, a new shirt, or a new car. Other times, we believe that indulging in our impulses will bring us happiness. While these things in themselves are not bad, it is worth asking ourselves whether any of these things have brought us true, lasting happiness.

Twin studies have shown that about 50 percent of happiness is based on genetics. This means that there are certain predispositions to happiness, but it also signifies that half of our happiness is dependent on other factors. In another study (source provided later in the text), it was found that 10 percent of happiness is determined by our life circumstances, such as wealth, relationship status, health, etc. This means that if 50 percent of our happiness can be attributed to genetic makeup and 10 percent to circumstances, there remains 40 percent of our happiness that is within our control and can be created by ourselves.

This 40 percent means that we have a significant influence on how happy we are in our lives. Not everything is left to chance, whims of others, or intentions. We have choice and free will. What does this have to do with gratitude? It turns out that research has shown that grateful people are indeed happier. Gratitude can reduce the frequency and duration of depressive episodes, which makes sense because it is difficult to feel bitterness, anger, envy, hostility, and resentment when you feel grateful. By its nature, gratitude has the ability to block more negative and unpleasant emotions. When it comes to gratitude, it is important to realize that the feelings you experience are valuable, and they all serve to direct you toward one goal.

Feeling fear, you may become anxious. This emotion puts your body in a state of vigilance, so you are prepared for anything and can adapt to your environment. It is very important to feel anxiety when you walk down a poorly lit street at night—emotions can help you maintain safety. Similarly, the feeling of anxiety before a public speaking engagement can encourage you to prepare for the event in the right way, such as creating an excellent presentation.

Emotions that are usually labeled as negative are simply more unpleasant. Bitterness, sadness, guilt, regret, shame, envy, resentment, and anxiety are not necessarily bad, but they can be uncomfortable, especially when they come back like a boomerang and are frequently experienced. Your mind may be programmed to focus on these emotions and pay them more attention. That's because they are significant emotions as they provide valuable information about yourself and how you respond to your environment. Without these emotions, you wouldn't know if there is danger lurking around the corner or if you are witnessing something that goes against your moral and ethical beliefs. These particular emotions can prompt you to take action. The downside is that you can quickly get stuck in them while living in your shadow.

Gratitude and positive emotions do not exclude negative experiences, but they can help maintain the right perspective and refrain from getting stuck in an uncomfortable emotional situation. Practicing gratitude is one way to transform your experiences into more positive emotions and improve your relationships with people, animals, and nature.

**The benefits of gratitude**

Have also been proven to increase our ability to experience a greater number of positive emotions. Gratitude is often associated with feelings such as love, compassion, humility, comfort, passion, and self-assurance. Cultivating gratitude can be a direct way to strengthen these emotions in your life.

Another benefit that comes from many studies is that grateful people are more resilient to stress. By finding the ability to be grateful for the things you have in your life, you are able to navigate challenges and difficulties much more quickly and effectively. Gratitude helps us recognize our strength, open our hearts, and fully experience life.

The good news is that you don't have to go through a crisis to notice gratitude. Gratitude is an opportunity waiting for you in every passing second.

Gratitude can be learned. Therefore, practicing gratitude can be a choice and a deliberate way of looking at the world. This does not mean that you should discount or diminish the difficulties or painful experiences in your life, but you should decide not to be overwhelmed by them in the present moment and find a way to transcend them. You can look at what you learn about others and yourself with gratitude as you navigate the struggles of everyday life.

# CHAPTER 5

## Mindfulness and meditation are closely related to gratitude

It's amazing how often we take someone else's emotional story as our own. When we hear it and identify with it, we start falling into the same patterns. Whether it's a habit or a specific way, to some extent, we all copy the habits and behaviors of those closest to us. While it's not necessarily a bad thing, as we can gain greater awareness from it, if we don't know that we're doing something or why we're doing it, it can be difficult to determine how it may impact our relationships and experiences with others. How can we recognize these patterns and "borrowed" behaviors?

How can we transition from less effective patterns to nurturing a mindset of gratitude? There are many ways to make progress in this direction, but to build awareness, the best path is through mindfulness practice. The simplest and clearest definition of mindfulness is nothing more than "paying attention on purpose." By practicing mindfulness, you focus on the details of your purpose and experience of that one chosen thing. You can be mindful of everything—your breath, eating, even cleaning the floor. Being mindful is simply noticing the experience of something happening in the present moment.

Mindfulness exercises can help in the treatment and prevention of depression. Taking time for deliberate attention can change the imbalance of chemical circuits in the brain and assist in transitioning to positive thought patterns. Studies have shown that mindful practices can improve overall body functioning, initiate healing processes, and contribute to well-being. It also allows for better relationships with others, as practicing mindfulness enables you to better recognize nonverbal cues

29

from others and engage in faster interactions.

When our lives become dynamic, busy, and hectic, we tend to rely on autopilot, losing attentiveness to stimuli. We also forget about gratitude. Sometimes we even yearn for what we're experiencing in the moment. Devoting a few minutes each day to pausing, slowing down, and harmonizing the body and mind can have a profound impact on how we feel in a given day and what we do to fill it.

**Living mindfully day by day**

Our thoughts, emotions, and behaviors are interconnected. Each feeds off the other and shapes our experiences in a similar, yet distinct way within the world we live. Practicing mindfulness helps us see experiences, relationships, and the environment around us in a different context. Through mindfulness practice, we can direct attention to our thoughts, behaviors, and emotions without judging them as good or bad. When we are mindful, we begin to see our world and perceive more existing possibilities within it. Every daily routine, task, or activity can become an opportunity to practice mindfulness and gratitude. You can practice mindful gratitude anywhere, at any time.

**Practicing mindfulness through meditation**

If you struggle with incorporating mindfulness into your daily life, you can use meditation to train your brain to do it automatically. Mindfulness can be cultivated through mindfulness meditation, which is a systematic method of focusing your attention. You can learn to meditate on your own, following instructions in books or using videos and tapes.

Some types of meditation primarily involve concentration, such as repeating phrases or focusing on the sensation of breath. This concentration allows for a continuous flow of thoughts that inevitably arise to come and go. Concentration meditation techniques and other activities can induce a relaxation response, which in turn can help reduce the body's response to stress.

## First steps with mindfulness meditation

Mindfulness meditation is based on concentration practices. Once you've achieved concentration, you begin observing the flow of your inner thoughts, emotions, and bodily sensations without judging them as good or bad.

Then, you start opening your mind and noticing the external experiences around you, such as sights, sounds, and touch, that make up the experience from moment to moment. The challenge in mindfulness meditation is not to focus on a specific idea, sensation, or emotion or become entangled in thoughts of the past or future. Instead, you should observe what comes to mind to discover which mental habits bring a sense of well-being or suffering.

There will be moments when you won't feel that this process is relaxing at all. However, over time, it will provide you with better opportunities to discover happiness and self-awareness. It will broaden your perspective by offering a broader range of experiences.

## Practicing gratitude meditation

Gratitude meditation is one of the most impactful and fulfilling exercises you can engage in. When you're able to cultivate a mindset of gratitude, you can start feeling more content with your life and achieve true happiness. Gratitude can make you feel good, and meditation can help you reach a deep state of relaxation and contemplation.

Gratitude meditation can be done together, or you can spend a few minutes at the beginning of a meditation session taking deep breaths and thinking about all the things you're grateful for in your life.

You can start practicing gratitude meditation by dedicating a few moments to perform relaxation techniques using deep breathing. "Start by sitting in a comfortable chair with your back straight and your feet flat on the floor. Rest your hands gently on your knees. Slowly breathe in through your nose, filling your lungs completely, and allowing your abdomen to expand with the inhalation. Try to hold the breath in your lungs and count to two. Then, exhale slowly and allow your abdomen to return to its natural position. At the end of the exhalation, pause briefly" (Declutter Your Mind, S.J. Scott, B. Davenport). You'll be supplying your body with a healthy dose of oxygen, which will help you feel significantly more relaxed.

When you're ready, sit in a comfortable position suitable for meditation and close your eyes. Allow your muscles to relax. Let your thoughts flow freely as you observe them. When you feel at ease and comfortable, begin thinking about everything you're grateful for in your life. The more grateful you are, the more you will receive in your life. Whether you choose to practice gratitude meditation or gratitude relaxation and regular breathing, you will become happier and healthier.

# CHAPTER 6

# Balance in gratitude

So far, you have discovered that gratitude has many positive qualities and benefits. You have learned that grateful people are happier, healthier, and more satisfied with their relationships. Gratitude opens us up to the possibility of connecting with others and can help us eliminate stressful situations and experiences. However, it's important to understand that every light casts a shadow, and gratitude is no exception.

For gratitude to exist in our relationships, there needs to be an exchange between us. There must be a giver and a receiver, and the exchange itself must be conducted consciously. When awareness of this gift is absent, the exchange becomes imbalanced. This can result in missed opportunities for gratitude or the expression of false gratitude.

Imbalanced gratitude or unhealthy recognition arises when there is a feeling that gratitude should be present, even when it's not. I have a thought that allows me to experience this: "I know I should be grateful, but I can't help but feel it, which triggers feelings of guilt or awkwardness or another form of unease."

## Surface-level gratitude

Surface-level gratitude is one that is not authentic and doesn't flow from the heart. It often occurs when there is a public expectation or demand for immediate confirmation of gratitude. The best example of this is the annual award shows broadcast on television. The words of gratitude are present, but the sentiment behind those words doesn't exist.

The emotion associated with this type of gratitude is rarely uplifting.

There are no additional benefits associated with other emotions that are often connected to gratitude, such as joy, happiness, love, connection, and even hope. Instead, superficial expressions of gratitude are often associated with feelings of unease and resentment.

You may also encounter surface-level gratitude when there are too many people thanking you. In an effort not to exclude anyone, you lose the essence of mindfulness. There can be a long list of acknowledgments recited without relevance to what is truly appreciated. The sense of recognition becomes diluted and less meaningful. This creates many situations where you may feel obligated to express thanks, even if you don't feel the emotions that could lead you to genuine gratitude, but rather to false gratitude.

## Obligatory gratitude

Obligatory gratitude bears some resemblance to surface-level gratitude. After all, there is an overwhelming sense of "should" rather than genuine appreciation. This type of gratitude often arises when you feel the need to say "thank you" for kindness received but one that wasn't needed or required. You may feel compelled to show gratitude when you feel obligated to thank someone for a gift you didn't want or like or when someone does something for you, and you wanted to do it yourself.

## Restoring balance

We have all, at one time or another, experienced imbalanced gratitude. The most important thing to understand is that it's not true gratitude. Whether false gratitude arises from cultural expectations or the intention to be perceived as better than others, it lacks essential components necessary for gratitude to thrive in your life. If you are engaged in an imbalanced gratitude exchange, it's up to you to seek and find a way to restore balance.

# CHAPTER 7

## How does gratitude work?

Psychologically, practicing gratitude allows us to become happier, more positive, and inclined to find joy and pleasure in everything we do. Expressing gratitude for what we have and those around us also has social benefits as we become more generous and engaged in our connection with the world.

Research has shown that gratitude benefits us both psychologically and physically. Physically, when we practice gratitude in our lives, it can help boost our immune system, leading to a healthier and more energetic life. It can reduce the likelihood of falling ill and enable us to lead a more active life.

Gratitude can empower you to better understand that life is about moments lived, not a constant pursuit of good or bad moments. It teaches us to be grateful for all the moments that make up our lives.

Take, for example, the case of someone who has just experienced a car accident, resulting in hospitalization and a leg cast. Now, instead of complaining about being in the hospital for a few weeks, this person is grateful for their life being saved. Being given a bonus by life, they can utilize this time to catch up on reading, focus on self-care, and personal development.

**Become more optimistic**

Gratitude can help you develop an optimistic and positive outlook on life by leveraging all the ups and downs. Living with gratitude allows you to understand and appreciate that being kind with unwavering patience is the key to your happiness, contentment, and peace. Instilling an attitude of gratitude from an early age helps you appreciate the blessings you have. It also helps you distance yourself from the current plague of overwhelm and distractions that affect so many people. Today, children often take things for granted too easily. This lack of gratitude puts them on a path that makes it difficult for them to find inner peace and satisfaction, which can negatively impact their ability and quality of forming relationships in their lives, both at work and at home.

## Become more thankful

The best thing about the empowering nature of gratitude is that it allows you to see yourself in a new light. The more grateful you are for everything that is good in your life, the more you will develop in those aspects of personal life that are insufficient for you. Gratitude makes you a more empathetic person who can appreciate the achievements of others without feeling envy. This can free you from focusing on doing things in your life that work for you.

## Gain more energy

Among the many beautiful ways in which gratitude can strengthen your life is the way it fuels you. Simply accepting the positive and letting go of the negative can make you look at your life with hope and optimism, which adds motivation to give your best in everything you do.

Gratitude is like the sun breaking through the window and illuminating the room when we open the curtains in the morning. Each of us has a need to experience such an important catalyst that can bring an exciting miracle into our lives.

## Find meaning in life

Life is more than a constant pursuit of material goods and achieving goals. Having a sense of gratitude for what we have and desiring the best for everyone else puts us on the path of self-realization, allowing us to cultivate contentment as a constant element of our lives. It also enables us to reach out to those who may need our help.

## Open up to friendship

People who practice gratitude have more positive energy and seem to be more popular due to their pleasant and courteous personality. This can help you gain more friends and have deeper, more meaningful connections in your relationships. Overall, grateful people are more helpful, sociable, and trusting.

# CHAPTER 8

# How to learn gratitude

Fortunately, gratitude is something you can learn. With the right practice and discipline, you can cultivate an attitude of gratitude in your life. The essence of gratitude lies in the fact that most people are unable to embrace the challenge when everything is going well. However, when a crisis arises or an unfortunate situation occurs, people fail to see a reason to be grateful. Many would rather complain about their lives. The essence of gratitude, however, is that it is nothing more than a state of mind. If you choose to, you can find a reason for gratitude even in those dark moments.

No matter how terrible things may happen to you, there is always something to be grateful for. It's important to remember that we are all on this planet for a short time, and as long as we are alive and breathing, there is something to celebrate. If something goes wrong, you must remember that you have the power to fix it. When you take some time to observe the behavior of grateful people, you will start to notice certain similarities in their attitudes.

**Have realistic expectations from life**

Life rarely goes the way we expect it to. The top students in school don't necessarily reach great heights in life. There are numerous cases where someone less talented than you can land a desired job or achieve greater success than you. No one knows what kind of cards we will be dealt in life. When you are prepared for the surprises that life inevitably throws your way, you will always be able to find a silver lining that leads you to gratitude.

## Dwell in unconditional happiness

When you place conditions on your happiness, you will likely never achieve that happiness. If you desire a specific sports car, that's okay, but if you were to decide that you have depression until you obtain it, what would happen if it were suddenly discontinued? People who willingly express gratitude for the good they see in their lives, regardless of its magnitude, are the ones who find it easy to be happy. Unconditional gratitude is definitely one of the prerequisites for a happy life.

## Accept that good comes from bad

People who can appreciate that good comes from bad discover that their hearts are grateful for the good in life, while also realizing and understanding that glitches and flaws will likely occur. They know that when they bask in the warm glow of the summer sun, the gloomy frost of winter is just around the corner. And conversely, when it rains, they know it's only a matter of time before the sun powers up their mighty batteries.

## Grow in optimism

People who find it easy to express gratitude for even the smallest of joys are not bothered by changes in life. They are eternal optimists who need the smallest glimmer of hope to be happy and content. For them, tomorrow is another day for birth and growth.

# CHAPTER 9

# Creating habits of gratitude

Gratitude is something that gives us infinite possibilities to experience every day. The challenge is to not become susceptible to the negative mindset of our brain. A negative mindset increases the tendency to focus on more uncomfortable emotions such as fear, anxiety, anger, and sadness. These emotions are necessary as they prompt us to pay attention to things that may be threatening or dangerous, but we shouldn't live in them or let them be the emotions that inform all of our life experiences.

Through the practice of gratitude, you can develop new thought patterns and new ways of experiencing your life. Similar to starting a new diet or exercise routine, engaging in a new behavior for an hour, a day, or a week will not result in long-term change. It is only through regular practice that sustainable change can be created. What you do consistently and frequently can quickly become a habit, something you do automatically.

Regardless of the situation, there is always an opportunity for gratitude. Even the most frustrating experiences can provide you with a chance to exercise gratitude, but they can also allow you to observe it and be influenced by its presence.

**Developing Habits**

Every new behavior or routine takes some time to develop into a new habit. When you first start driving, everything is new and requires full attention. When you start a new fitness plan, it takes some effort and commitment. Over time, the novelty becomes something you simply do. This process is usually subtle and often requires some support or encouragement.

Developing a habit of gratitude will require some effort on your part. Shifting gratitude into a consistent practice requires diligence, but it is a worthwhile energy investment. Research has shown that, in addition to increasing awareness of the abundance already present in your life, practicing gratitude provides a wide range of benefits, including:

•improved ability to cope with daily stress,
•increased optimism compared to the past,
•expanded sense of connection with people and the world,
•increased resilience to traumatic events,
•enhanced sense of well-being,
•boosted physical activity,
•improved sleep quality,
•enhanced physical health,
•reduced anxiety,
•positive impact on cardiovascular and immune system functions.

It's important to remember that developing habits of gratitude takes time. There may be days when you completely forget about gratitude. That's okay. You can resume the practice the next day. Over time, the practice of gratitude becomes more automated. It's like learning something new—you have to be patient. By continuing the practice, you will notice that the rewards in your life will sprout like mushrooms after rain.

## Practice Giving

By harnessing the practical power of this message, simply share what you have. You will unleash waves of well-being driven by the joy of action without reason or cause. When you believe that everything and everyone owes you, how can you be grateful or experience the magical power of gratitude? This belief deserves to break down the wall that blocks gratitude.

So, the question arises, how can you transition from a mindset of entitlement to a practice of gratitude? There are several ways to achieve this. First, start by adjusting your own attitude and modeling a grateful mindset at home and with yourself. You can also infect your children with the idea of gratitude and giving, rather than entitlement and receiving. The key to deepening gratitude is engaging in actions and interactions that focus on sharing, giving, and connecting, rather than doing something to get something back.

This is an unconditional action that flows from the depths of our hearts. This particular action allows you to avoid frustration and feelings of lack. Believing that the world owes you everything is a false assumption that will only lead to disappointment, tension in your relationships, and further resentment and frustration.

## Record Gratitude

When seeking ways to amplify and support gratitude in your life, you can utilize the simple act of keeping gratitude journals. Often, when people talk about writing thank-you notes, they think back to a time when they were obligated to write obligatory thanks for graduations, birthdays, weddings. In such situations, writing thank-you notes may feel a bit discouraging and overwhelming. In many of those situations, the received gifts are not obligatory, but the thanks are primarily crafted due to a sense of social responsibility and therefore a compulsion to express gratitude. While this may not be representative of genuine gratitude, it is a positive step towards developing habits of gratitude because it is a way of acknowledging the received gifts.

From there, you can take it a step further and move beyond obligatory gratitude and into reflective gratitude. Reflective gratitude occurs when you are able to step back from a situation, recall the event, and re-experience the emotions that occurred at that moment or time. Often, we don't realize the benefits we receive from someone until we take the time to reflect.

Thank-you notes have a positive impact on those who receive them. Taking the time to consider the relationships you have cultivated and the gifts those relationships offer, you can shift from a place of resentment or dissatisfaction to a feeling of gratitude for the gifts received. It also allows you to stimulate the possibility of considering the people around you and their influence on you.

CHAPTER 10

# Cultivating gratitude in your life

Now you have the opportunity to practice cultivating gratitude in your life, whether alone or with others. The art lies in the practice. Like any new skill you learn, developing a gratitude mindset takes time. By incorporating the following practices into your daily life, you will find that over time, you experience the world a little differently. You will start to see opportunities hiding in the most obvious places and notice the richness in your relationships, feeling more connected to the world around you.

Not all of these practices will feel comfortable to you, and some may even make you feel a little silly. That's okay; allow yourself to embrace them. Try them out. Some of these exercises will resonate with you, while others may not. The key to cultivating gratitude and achieving greatness is to practice until it becomes intuitive.

The first few practices involve meditation. As I discussed earlier, meditation and mindfulness are key aspects of finding gratitude in everyday life. If you are not familiar with the practice of meditation, these exercises may be a bit challenging. If your thoughts start to wander or your mind shifts into judgment and interrogation mode, that's okay; simply redirect your focus to the practice, to what is within your reach. It is important to be gentle with yourself. There is no right or wrong way to do these exercises. It is the practice that will make you a master.

**Gratitude Meditation Practice**

Begin this practice by sitting calmly in a comfortable chair. If you don't mind closing your eyes, do so. If not, you can simply soften your gaze, directing it to the floor about three feet in front of you.

Calm your mind and gently shift your attention by focusing on your breath. Take a deep breath in through your nose, drawing the air deeply into your heart. Try to envision your heart being filled to the brim, radiating with purple light. As you inhale, visualize soft, warm, pink light filling your heart, gently merging with the purple light that fills the space within your chest.

As you exhale through your mouth, softly releasing the breath, visualize a gentle blue light transitioning from the purple light into your body.

With each inhale, silently say to yourself, "I am full of gratitude."

With each exhale, silently say to yourself, "I offer gratitude to the universe."

Continue this cycle for four minutes. After the time is up, gently open your eyes, raising your gaze from the floor.

**Gratitude Chronicles Practice and Meditation**

For this exercise, you will need a journal or the Gratitude Chronicles that I have created for you. You can now get them by visiting the website: [insert website link here].

Every evening, before going to bed, focus your attention by directing it to your breath and maintaining a relaxed posture.

If you feel comfortable, close your eyes or squint your gaze, directing it to a fixed point on the ground about three feet in front of you.

Take a few deep breaths, paying attention to the inhale and exhale.

Reflect on the events of the day. Visualize those events as they occurred, remembering to pay particular attention to moments that contained acts of kindness, laughter, and beauty. As you notice these events, pay attention to how your body feels. Notice the sensations you experienced at that moment. What thoughts arise in your mind?

After reviewing the day, gently shift your focus back to your breath. Open your eyes and write down your observations in your journal.

**Gratitude Chronicles Practice**

Start noticing things that happen each day for which you are grateful. These things can be big or small—it doesn't matter. The size of what you identify is not essential for effectively practicing gratitude. Instead, you are noticing things you can appreciate throughout the day. You can be grateful for a person, for opportunities presented to you, for a good cup of coffee or tea, or maybe for the day coming to an end and preparing for rest in your bed under your favorite bedding.

Every night before going to sleep, write down the things you were grateful for throughout the day. Remember: they can be big or small—it doesn't matter. Write down at least three things each day, and once a week, sit down and review your journal entries.

## Breath and Gratitude

Even on the busiest days, there are small moments when you can practice gratitude. Take a moment, two, or three times a day to slow down and focus your full attention on your breath.

Notice each breath. Observe each inhale and exhale, noticing that at this moment, you don't have to do anything but breathe. As your breath captures your attention, silently say the words "thank you" with each exhale, which should be between five and eight breaths, as a gentle reminder that at this moment, you are present and grateful for the gift of your breath and the fortune of being alive.

Practice this at least three times a week. It would be great if you could continue such practice every day, three times a day.

## Gratitude Reminders

It is very easy to forget about something, especially when you are trying to create a new habit. Placing visual reminders around your main area or workspace can help you stay on track with your goals. Create reminders that encourage you throughout the day to think about gratitude or simply to pause and reflect. Here are a few ideas for gratitude reminders:

•Carry a small stone in your pocket. When you notice the stone, take a moment to pause and think about gratitude.
•Place a note on your office wall, the fridge at home, or the mirror in the bathroom that says, "I am grateful."
•Set an alarm on your phone to go off once or a few times a day as a prompt to stop and reflect on gratitude.
•Schedule a five-minute "gratitude visit" in your office calendar at least two or three times a week. Use the reminder feature in your calen-

dar to help you stay on track with the practice.

•Have a "gratitude partner," someone you check in with every day to help identify aspects of gratitude throughout the day.

## Family Gratitude Practice

You don't have to practice gratitude alone. After all, gratitude is about relationships and connections. You can create a culture of gratitude at home as a family activity.

Create a gratitude list for your family.

Place a board or sheet of paper on the fridge or in another easily accessible location and invite all members of your family to contribute to it each day. The items on the list can be big or small—it doesn't matter.

Choose one day a week to share the list during a family meal.

Create a new list each week.

## Gratitude Letter Practice

There is always an opportunity to express appreciation and gratitude, even if it has been years. Reflecting on people in your life for whom you feel grateful but haven't yet thanked can be a powerful means of nurturing gratitude.

Write a letter to that person, expressing your appreciation for them. Let them know how they have impacted your life. If possible, hand-deliver the letter and read it aloud before giving it to them.

## Thank You - Gratitude Chronicles

Similar to a thank-you letter, the Gratitude Chronicles are a fascinating expression of gratitude. They allow you, as the recipient, to enjoy the gift/benefit and authenticate the person who brought the experience into your life, making it recognizable and appreciated.

Arrange a box of thank-yous and get into the habit of writing gratitude scripts. Keep them neatly stored, thus creating one of the chapters of the Akashic Chronicles, from which someone now and in the future can draw power. The power of gratitude that you were able to show to someone who did something valuable for you.

# CHAPTER 11

# Practice and knowledge will make you a master

Thank you for reaching this point. I have tried to sincerely explain why the concept of gratitude is so important to me and why it deserves attention. And I believe you feel the value of this message. I will now share what I have experienced in my practices, exercises, and it goes like this: knowledge without practical application has no value. After introducing this, now comes the most important moment of our meeting. I have prepared materials specifically for you that will allow you to reach the heights of your achievements. I also wish for you to quickly achieve a vibration frequency exceeding 700 on the Scale of Consciousness (it is worth familiarizing yourself with Dr. Hawkins' Map of Consciousness Level). Practice, savor, enjoy the practice, affirm. Experience love, joy, happiness, and abundance in every area of your life through these practices. Let's get to work.

**I start my day with Gratitude**

I begin each day with a feeling of love and gratitude in my heart. I avoid negative thoughts that bring my day down to a harmful level.

I see each new day as an opportunity to give thanks to the universe.

I count the blessings that surround me and fill my life. I appreciate the people who make my life easier and better.

I am grateful for my friends and family every morning.

I am grateful for my work, home, neighborhood, and relationships.

I see others suffering around me and focus on peace.

Gratitude fills my spirit, and my joy increases.

I appreciate the five senses that help me experience a connection with our planet. I enjoy being able to connect with nature, people, and animals.

My morning is complete because gratitude occupies my thoughts. I take advantage of each morning to appreciate the value of my life and the achievements that come from it.

I reflect on my experiences and the past. I influence my actions now for the future, so I can experience abundance in every area of my life. I focus on ideas that help us all grow and effectively achieve new goals.

Today, I started my morning with gratitude and peace in my mind. I see how my attitude affects my entire day, so my morning is a time for reflection.

**Self-reflection questions:**

How can I find time in the morning to express gratitude?
In what ways can I teach my family to cultivate gratitude every morning?
What can I do to eliminate negative thoughts and experiences that may impact my mornings?

# I am grateful for being able to experience another day

Every day is unique and brings blessings and new experiences. Even those days that may seem negative have valuable lessons to offer. x e-re are many subtle reasons to be grateful for each day.

Every day is another opportunity to share time and experiences with those I love. x e closeness of my friends and family sustains me in difficult situations and brings more smiles to my face. Every day I can spend with those I love is precious.

Living for another day means I can enjoy the beauty of nature, which is ever-changing and a constant source of wonder for me. I feel peaceful and fulfilled when I experience the natural world.

Each morning, I wake up in anticipation of what today holds for me. I cannot predict what life may bring, and that is what makes my life so intriguing.

Another day on Earth is another day of joy! I understand that life is short and passes quickly. I am determined to make the most of each day. I am free from worries and cares. x e prospect of experiencing another day fills me with excitement.

Today, I look forward to another interesting and meaningful day. I use my time wisely and enjoy the process of life. I face challenges with a smile in my soul and on my face. I am grateful for being able to experience another day.

**Self-reflection questions:**

What have I learned from difficult times in my life?
When have I felt hopeless in the past? Why did things eventually improve?
What should I expect in my life?

# Fan the flames of gratitude to create a positive shift in your life

Consistent gratitude is one of the most powerful tools you can use to make your world brighter tomorrow. However, gratitude is not a magical shortcut. It may not bring about any external changes other than those happening within you. Yet, what gratitude can do is open you up to other possibilities.

When you become aware of the multitude of blessings already present in your life, you can increasingly focus on abundance. This can put you on the path to a mentally rich state filled with optimism.

This transformation occurs when you begin expressing genuine gratitude to others and start feeling grateful for everything in your life that brings you joy.

## Stay attuned to abundance

A great way to increase awareness of the abundance you already have is by engaging with the Chronicles of Gratitude Land. You don't have to wait for something extraordinary to happen in your life to appreciate it. Instead, open your journal once a day and take a few minutes to write down everything you are grateful for.

You can feel grateful for all the experiences you encounter, even the small ones. On days when you think you have absolutely nothing to appreciate, you can create a collection of small things. For example, pay attention to the air you breathe or the food in your pantry.

As you realize there are so many things to be grateful for, you will find yourself thinking about an increasing number of blessings in your life. After several weeks of continuing to make notes in this way, you may find that you spontaneously shift onto the "path of success."

Some New Age gurus may tell you that your newfound happiness is a result of "positive vibrations." Instead, it likely has more to do with training your brain and recognizing opportunities. You have convinced your subconscious that you are riding a wave of abundance. Why not?

You deserve it!

## Gratitude as a tool

Gratitude can make you a stronger person. Use gratitude as a tool to arm yourself for negative and challenging times. Focus on what you have rather than what you lack.

A study published in the Journal of Personality and Social Psychology titled "Counting Blessings Versus Burdens: An Experimental Investigation of Gratitude and Subjective Well-Being in Daily Life" found that those who maintained a grateful attitude experienced greater physical and psychological well-being.

Research suggests that daily gratitude enhances self-esteem, decreases materialism, envy, and egocentric tendencies. Gratitude can also help foster meaningful relationships and generate social capital. People who consistently express gratitude are more positively oriented than those who do not.

Further studies suggest that when you cultivate gratitude, you are more likely to grow in response to stress, rather than shrink.

By encoding in your mind what you are grateful for, you can reduce stress. As you actively deal with stressors, others will notice your new positive qualities.

All these effects come together to create new possibilities in your life that you otherwise would not have noticed. So, go ahead, start keeping your Chronicles of Gratitude Land, and let stress dissolve. Open yourself to the possibility of abundance. You will be glad you did!

# 5 benefits of keeping a Gratitude Land Chronicle

## Increase positivity

When you write down things you are grateful for in your life, you naturally become more optimistic and confident. Focusing on the goodness in your life gives less power to negative emotions and more power to positive ones. While positive thoughts may flow through your mind throughout the day, taking the time to write them down makes them more concrete.

## Improve sleep

Spending a few minutes before bed to write down things you are grateful for can calm your mind and alleviate any anxieties that arise during the day. A calm and grateful mind will help you fall asleep faster. Gratitude has been shown to induce a relaxation response and has been proven to be a powerful sleep aid.

## Enhance self-esteem

When you focus on the negative aspects of your life, it's easy to feel overwhelmed. We often hold ourselves to higher standards than we do others, but keeping a Gratitude Land Chronicle can help you focus on your own accomplishments. Expressing gratitude can help limit the natural tendency we have to compare ourselves to others, which can be detrimental to our self-esteem. When you express gratitude for what you have, you will experience less resentment and envy towards others and have a greater sense of self-worth.

## Reduce stress

By focusing on feelings of contentment and satisfaction, you naturally counteract stress. While you will still have to deal with challenges in your life, practicing gratitude will help you cope with them better.

## Improve health

Grateful people live healthier and longer lives than their ungrateful counterparts. This is because they have the motivation to take better care of themselves. Grateful individuals experience fewer ailments and are more inclined towards healthy eating and physical exercise.

These are just a few of the many benefits of keeping a Gratitude Land Chronicle. If you don't have one yet, start creating it today, and you can live a happier and healthier life from now on.

# Simple exercises to start practicing gratitude today

When you get used to performing at a high level, you overlook the little things in life that make it worth living. Eventually, you fail to appreciate the blessings in your life and forget to soak in precious moments with your loved ones. Practicing gratitude can not only help you feel more grounded and peaceful, but also enhance your ability to share love with others.

Here are a few simple gratitude exercises that can make you happier:

**Exercise 1**

Identify three things you appreciate. Take a moment to identify three things in your life that you are grateful for and hold in high regard. These things can be based on the present, past, or future. While no category or item is too big or small, it's important to be specific and feel it in your gratitude.

**Exercise 2**

Identify three things you perceive as given. We often take things for granted in our lives. Take some time to reflect on those things and discover which ones you value the most. It could be anything. You might take for granted that you're in good physical health or that you have a well-paying job.

**Exercise 3**

Identify three things you appreciate about yourself. Due to our constant need for comparison, this can be challenging. Take some time to think about things you value about yourself. They could include your personality, daily actions, qualities, or anything else directly related to you.

**Exercise 4**

Identify three things that help you be grateful in the present moment. To cultivate gratitude, it's necessary to be present. Take the time to reflect on what you can appreciate in your current situation. Think about the time you dedicate to your health, the environment around you, or anything else that relates to the present moment.

## Exercise 5

Identify three people who are significant in your life. Think about all the people you have encountered in your life. They can be coaches, teachers, mentors, family members, friends. Reach out to those individuals and take some time to reflect on how they have impacted your life.

## Exercise 6

Create thank-you cards. Create thank-you cards for those three individuals who have influenced your life. You don't have to send them; the act of expressing your gratitude will be beneficial for your personal growth in this area.

Practicing these six exercises regularly will help you develop gratitude and lead you towards a healthier and happier life.

# Good things are happening in my life

Every morning, I count my blessings. I am filled with gratitude because I believe that only positive things are happening in my life. I am a happy person. I deserve positive things to happen in my life. I am blessed.

Whenever I feel uneasy, I remind myself of the wonderful things I experience every day. I can quickly list many things in my life that are amazing and worthy of gratitude.

Reminding myself of my own blessings keeps me in a positive vibration and improves my mood. I can change my mood by focusing on the good things happening in my life.

I work diligently every day to ensure that I deserve a fantastic life. Good things are more likely to happen when I do my part and take action.

I avoid relying on luck because I am the happiest person I know. Good things simply seem to happen when I least expect them.

Even the negative aspects of my life are improving every day. This improvement transforms negativity into positive energy. Improvement is more significant and more attainable than perfection.

Today, I bask in my happiness. I strive to stimulate my mind and spirit today by appreciating my life. Many good things are happening in my life right now. I am confident that even more good things will come.

**Self-reflection questions:**

What are three great things in my life? Why do I appreciate them?
What happens when I solely focus on my challenges? Why do I sometimes focus on the negatives? Do I believe it helps?
If I paid more attention to the positive things in my life, what would likely be the outcome of that action?

# 7 ways to practice Gratitude

When you're facing a challenging situation, it can be difficult to see the positives. This is where gratitude can help. It doesn't mean you're grateful for the difficulties, but you should express gratitude for the positive things happening in your life, even if they are small. Gratitude can help you see your current situation in a way that reduces panic and opens your thinking to new solutions in the present moment.

Here are 7 ways to practice gratitude:

## Exercise 1

Take a moment to view your daily world through the lens of gratitude. When you start looking at things with gratitude, you'll be amazed at how much goodness is present in your life that you probably take for granted.

## Exercise 2

Create a Gratitude Journal. Keeping a Gratitude Journal only requires dedicating a few moments at the end of the day to write down things you are grateful for in your life. You don't even need to buy a fancy notebook to reap the benefits.

## Exercise 3

If you identify something or someone in your life with a negative characteristic, change that characteristic in your mind to something more positive. For example, if you associate your conference room with a cold space, start thinking of it as a conference room with a beautiful view.

## Exercise 4

To practice and benefit from gratitude, you must also practice humility. Humility is defined as being modest and respectful. Take some time to examine where you can apply humility in your life.

## Exercise 5

Each day, give yourself at least one compliment. You can do this directly or by expressing appreciation for something in your life. It can be as simple as saying, "I love how quiet it is in the morning."

## Exercise 6

When you find yourself in a difficult situation, ask yourself what can I learn from this? Reflect on the situation without emotions, identify what you can be grateful for.

## Exercise 7

Take an oath not to criticize, complain, or gossip for a week. If you slip up, rally your willpower and keep going. Focus and dedicate time to notice how much energy you waste each day on negative thoughts.

You don't need any specialized equipment to practice gratitude. All you need to do is use your mind, heart, and simply want to do it.

# 5 surprising health benefits of Gratitude

Holidays or one-time incidents are not the only times when you should practice gratitude. The powerful benefits of gratitude come from incorporating it into year-round habits. To enjoy the many mental and physical health benefits of gratitude, all it takes is a little introspection.

Here are 5 surprising health benefits of gratitude:

## Benefit #1: Increased patience

Researchers from Northeastern University found that people who were grateful for everyday things were more patient and able to make more rational decisions compared to those who did not feel gratitude on a daily basis.

## Benefit #2: Improved relationships

Feeling gratitude towards your partner, and vice versa, can improve various aspects of your relationship, according to recent research published in the Journal of Theoretical Social Psychology. This includes a stronger sense of connection and overall relationship satisfaction. Being grateful for yourself can significantly help in your love life as well.

## Benefit #3: Better sleep

Gratitude can help you sleep better and longer. This is likely due to having more positive thoughts before bedtime, which can help calm the nervous system. If you plan to make a daily gratitude list or keep a gratitude journal, it's best to do it right before sleep.

## Benefit #4: Alleviates depression

Gratitude is powerful. By practicing the "three good things" exercise daily, you can observe a significant improvement in low vibrations and overall happiness, sometimes within just a few weeks. The activity involves thinking about three good things or moments that happened during the day.

**Benefit #5: Gives you lasting happiness**

Many things can give you a happiness boost, from receiving a compliment to enjoying a sweet treat. Unfortunately, these types of instant gratifications can fade quickly and leave you wanting more. Gratitude, on the other hand, can lead to a more sustainable form of happiness because it's not based on immediate satisfaction but rather a state of mind. By taking the time to regularly express gratitude for things in your life, you are more likely to experience long-lasting happiness.

Gratitude doesn't require fancy exercise equipment, but it can significantly transform your life. By dedicating just a few minutes each day to express your gratitude, you can reap significant benefits for both your mental and physical health.

# How to Harness the Benefits of Gratitude

Gratitude is an attitude and a way of life that has many benefits for health, happiness, and contentment with everyday life. It goes hand in hand with mindfulness and focusing on appreciating what we have now, rather than constantly needing to have more.

Here are a few ways to harness the benefits of gratitude and enjoy a happier and healthier life:

**Think of someone who has helped you**

Take a few minutes to reflect on how someone has helped you in life. It could be a teacher, parent, mentor, or friend. Consider how you have benefited from their support. Then write them a heartfelt note, visit them, or give them a call to let them know how their support has improved your life. If you no longer have contact with that person, still make a note of it and keep the list as a reminder of gratitude.

**Notice while walking**

Take some time to walk in the garden or be in nature. As you walk, think about how nature helps sustain our lives and make us feel more comfortable and happy. Focus on gratitude for fresh air, beautiful flowers, or the shade of a tree.

**Think of someone who helps you daily**

It could be a parent, partner, beloved pet, best friend, or teacher. Spend a week observing them and focus on the various ways they make you happier and more comfortable in your life. Show your gratitude by doing something special for them.

**Share with others**

Gratitude stems from accepting that you are fortunate in your life. Sharing this with others who are less fortunate has a positive impact on everyone involved. Giving to others is a wonderful way to express gratitude for all the good things you have in your life.

## Choose to be grateful

Someone who is grateful sees everything in their life, both good and bad, as gifts. Being grateful means looking at failures and challenges as gifts from which you can learn. They understand that difficulties and setbacks provide them an opportunity to learn something they wouldn't have otherwise, and they are grateful for it.

Harnessing the power of gratitude doesn't mean that your life is problem-free. It's simply a way to influence your emotional state and energy levels to enhance productivity and satisfaction with life.

# 5 Tips for Maintaining Gratitude Journals

There are many proven benefits to keeping gratitude journals. The time you invest in purposeful thinking and writing about the things that fill you up can yield significant gains.

Here are 5 tips for maintaining gratitude journals:

## Make it a routine

Scientists have extensively studied the science behind habit formation. Keeping a gratitude journal as a way to feel happier in the long run must be part of your daily routine. Choose a time for journaling in your gratitude journal and set reminders for your practice to ensure daily writing. Write in your journal frequently enough to form a habit, but not so often that you become immune to the impact of what you're doing.

## Write in detail

Writing in your gratitude journal should not be another item to check off your to-do list. If you approach your gratitude journal in this way, you deny yourself the benefits you can gain from its practice. Be present and mindful of the notes you make. Remember to describe things in detail in your journal and deeply reflect on the things that have recently impacted your life.

## Embrace the negatives

You will never be able to completely escape life's challenges. Every number of difficulties can affect our sense of gratitude. However, if we try to rush through these struggles or fight hard for acknowledgment, we may end up fueling feelings of failure and unrest. So, when faced with challenges, allow yourself to taste the bitterness of the negatives. Find gratitude in unexpected moments: Challenge yourself to find positive aspects in the more difficult events of your life. The purpose of a gratitude journal is to savor the fruits of life, but there is even greater gratitude that you can discover. For example, were you preparing to go out only to find out your car had a flat tire? Find gratitude for not driving when the tire was damaged.

**Practice gratitude for the right things**

People who are consumers of material experiences and wealth are less likely to be satisfied compared to those who are grateful for what they currently have, according to studies. Instead of expressing gratitude for material possessions due to their ownership, focus on what these items give you.

Maintaining a gratitude journal will help you focus on the positive aspects of your life and make you happier and overall healthier.

# Every breath I take is a reminder of my blessings

Every morning and evening, I inhale blessings and exhale gratitude. The breath of air entering my body keeps me alive and awakens infinite possibilities. I cherish and appreciate the blessings of life and strength.

With each breath, I think of something I am grateful for. I can spend hours each day on this because the list is so long.

When I am in the presence of my friends and loved ones, I cultivate mindfulness to immerse myself in the present moment. I inhale their essence and the joy they bring to my life. Absorbing their spirit fills me with such peace and satisfaction.

I take in the positive energy that surrounds me. It uplifts and sustains me. It gives me a reason to navigate through the toughest times.

On challenging workdays, I take a moment to meditate on my accomplishments. I remind myself that although it may seem impossible today, my history shows that I overcome challenges.

I have enough, and I feel content.

Today, I am humbled by all the goodness that my life presents to me each day. There are so many reasons to be grateful. I say "thank you" for the blessings and my ability to share them with the world.

**Self-reflection questions:**

What blessings have I noticed today?
How can I give back all the blessings I receive?
For what material and spiritual things am I most grateful?

# 5 top tips to cultivate gratitude and increase happiness

In the face of pressures and demands of daily life, it can be a powerful challenge to pause and reflect on what we are grateful for. When we manage to do so, we can express gratitude for what we have and experience incredible benefits.

Here are 5 top tips to cultivate gratitude and increase happiness:

## Stop and look around

A simple way to cultivate the habit of gratitude is to take a moment during the day and ask yourself what you can be grateful for in your life, who are three people you can be grateful for in your life, and why. However, don't focus on the numbers—if you can only think of one person, that's okay. The key is to focus on a few moments and reflect on what you are grateful for in your life.

## Start with yourself

Look within and outside of yourself. Identify when you can cultivate the habit of being grateful, as this will lead to a significant increase in self-worth and self-confidence. Remember that gratitude doesn't have to be only about our achievements, but can also include the qualities we possess.

## Notice something small

You don't have to focus only on big and obvious things to be grateful for in your life. Also, think about smaller things that, in the puzzle of details, contribute to the whole. Open your eyes to the small, everyday details that you can appreciate. They allow you to see more simplicity in the beauty that surrounds us in life, especially what we have within ourselves.

## Do it spontaneously

The only way to develop the habit of gratitude is to stick to it and not let it become one of those things you forget about. To make gratitude a habit, it's best to spend a minute in the morning and find three things, big or small, that you are grateful for in your life. Then, each evening, take a few minutes to write down three to five things you are grateful for that day.

**Express your gratitude**

To truly increase your happiness, you need to express your gratitude. Make other people happier by showing them how grateful you are for their presence in your life. This will not only bring a smile to their faces, but also make you happier.

Cultivating gratitude doesn't require a lot of time or effort to become a habit. Taking even small steps to deepen your appreciation can increase your happiness.

# How cultivating a grateful attitude can improve your mental health

Gratitude is strongly linked to emotions that can help you enjoy better health and happiness. It plays a significant role in nurturing relationships and can even inspire better self-care.

Here's how cultivating a grateful attitude can improve your mental health and make you happier in life.

## Enhances the juiciness of happiness

When you integrate gratitude into your daily life, you strengthen the habit of adopting a more positive perspective and appreciating the small moments of everyday life. You become less prone to taking things for granted and become more open to experiencing the realm of small joys. Gratitude shields your mood from disappointment and helps you quickly notice the brighter side of your life. You focus on what you have and what is worth developing within yourself.

## Increases life satisfaction

Those who practice daily gratitude appear less materialistic and have greater hope in life. They are also more resilient to adversity and less likely to feel like victims when things don't go their way. Better coping with tragedies and crises can help improve the quality and experience of life.

## Improves mental and physical health

When you embrace gratitude, you have a lower likelihood of suffering from anxiety and depression. People who practice daily gratitude tend to be more optimistic and experience increased energy levels. Gratitude also has a positive impact on cardiovascular health and the immune system, effectively lowering blood pressure, increasing pain tolerance, and positively influencing pregnancy.

## Boosts self-esteem

Those who genuinely experience gratitude in their lives have higher levels of happiness and much greater self-confidence and self-worth. Being grateful directs your attention to happier, more positive thoughts, which can pave the way for feeling better about yourself and helping to alleviate negative panic.

**Elevates success levels**

Individuals with a grateful disposition have a higher likelihood of achieving their goals more quickly. Those in leadership positions report that expressing genuine gratitude and appreciation to colleagues improves team productivity and motivation.

Being grateful isn't always easy, but without it, life can be incredibly lonely, discouraging, and impoverished. Expressing gratitude can enrich and uplift your life, inspiring and transforming it.

# 4 tremendous ways to apply gratitude to change your life

It's amazing how one simple affirming action can make such a difference in our lives. One thing that can have a tremendous impact on your life is realizing the power of gratitude. Practicing gratitude can influence every aspect of your life and transform it for the better.

Here are 4 tremendous ways to apply gratitude to change your life:

## Shift out of a negative mood

Instead of getting angry at someone, express gratitude towards them. It may not always be easy, as it involves a significant shift in attitude. When someone is driving you crazy, rather than getting angry at them, focus on things you are grateful for. This practice can gradually change your mood. Expressing gratitude towards someone instead of anger not only improves your mood, but can also transform the relationship and improve its situation. See how the other person responds. :)

## Transform relationships

It is always important to communicate your problems with your spouse or others. Constantly criticizing and pointing out their flaws diminishes the quality of relationships. Instead, when you feel the need to criticize them, pause, take a deep breath, and calm down. Start thinking about all the reasons you are grateful for your partner, conversation companions, and then express your gratitude to them as soon as possible. Expressing gratitude will help strengthen your relationships.

## Mindfulness is the key to parenting

Many parents get frustrated with their children. Unfortunately, too often, by constantly conveying their frustrations to their children, they instill a sense of negativity in them. Instead of constantly criticizing them, take a moment to calm yourself and reflect on all the reasons you are grateful for your children. Share those reasons with your children and take the opportunity to teach them instead of criticizing them.

Both of you will be better off.

**Use adversity to cope with tragedy**

When you suffer from a tragedy, try to be grateful for the life you still have. It can be paralyzing in the face of catastrophes in your life, but by embracing change, you can overcome it. Even in sadness, you can find something even more valuable from the tragedy. Gratitude for the life you still have. Love for the people you constantly have around you and the appreciation for the fleeting beauty of life. Utilize the situation to express appreciation for the people around you and embrace life as it unfolds.

Recognizing and implementing practices to incorporate gratitude into the rhythm of your life will transform it for the better.

# Blessings follow me wherever I go

I am blessed in all things and choose to focus on the goodness in my life. Even in the face of challenging events, I always remember that I am blessed.

I always have an abundance of what I need. And often, I have more than enough. I am abundantly loved and have abundant love to give in return.

Infinite resources are at my fingertips. In the realm of finances, I always have enough to meet my basic needs and many of my other desires.

If I experience times when I feel a lack of abundance, I remind myself that I truly have everything I need. Whether I am employed or unemployed, in a partnership or single, have many children or no children, I feel blessed in numerous ways.

Nothing I can do can destroy or wash away the blessings that come to my mind. To fully satisfy my life, I just need to remember the abundance available to me.

My universe is vast, and my heart is filled with the radiant energy of unconditional love. Blessings come to me effortlessly, and I cultivate gratitude for them.

Today, I take the time to contemplate the ways in which I am blessed. I regularly experience gratitude for all the wonderful things in my life. And I seek opportunities to express that gratitude by living with a sense of abundance.

**Self-reflection questions:**

What blessings have I noticed today?
How can I give back all the blessings I receive? For what material and spiritual things am I most grateful?

# 5 ways to cultivate gratitude for a happier life

Some people believe that if they had more things or more luck, they would be more grateful. However, the number of things you accumulate does not determine your attitude. Gratitude is an attitude that can be easily cultivated, regardless of your current situation.

Here are five ways to cultivate gratitude for a happier life:

### Start a Gratitude Chronicle

Take a few moments each day to write down five things you are grateful for in your life. These things can range from being grateful for waking up in the morning to feeling rested and getting to work on time. Take a moment to feel how you are filled with positive energy, and let that feeling drive you towards a positive attitude for the rest of the day.

### Pause and Smell the Flowers

Change the way you think about your day by simply pausing and smelling the flowers for a moment. Actively try to catch the positive bug before you become overwhelmed with negative thoughts or emotions. Go for a walk and feel gratitude for the things surrounding you, such as the oxygen provided by the trees around you. This simple act can give you a fresh perspective on a stressful situation.

### Balance with Positive Thoughts

Before getting upset over what may seem like a challenging situation, take a moment to transform a negative thought into a positive one. If you find yourself stuck in negative experiences, which may seem like an endless moment, treat it as an opportunity for meditation or induce a calmer state before returning home.

### Bid Farewell to Complaining

Initiate a new style in your life by refraining from complaining for an entire day. Cultivate mindfulness to find one good thing among a dozen negative things that may affect you throughout the day. Allow yourself to transform through this new attitude.

## Compliment as the Key to Relationships

Share your kindness and genuine admiration with someone close to you, whether it's a friend or a stranger. Not only will it spread love to another person, but it will also uplift you and push you to focus on the good, allowing you to build even stronger positive relationships with the world.

By incorporating some of these gratitude exercises into your daily life, you will be able to expand your experiences, allowing you to be more deeply grateful for each moment and each day.

# My Personal Reflection...

I am grateful for all the possibilities. My attitude reflects my happiness.

I am grateful for all the possibilities that come to mind. I have let go of the idea that things have to be perfect for me to be happy. I understand that every situation presents both challenges and rewards.

Relying on a conflict-free life to feel good is a gift. There will always be challenges, and I cannot delay my happiness because of their presence.

I believe that success comes easily to those who take action with what they have at hand. Small successes often lead to bigger opportunities.

For this reason, I have decided to see possibilities in every circumstance. Even unpleasant situations can lead to better opportunities that wouldn't be available without facing the challenge.

I know that challenges teach me patience and other skills I need to make the most out of my life.

Obstacles help me grow.

I embrace all challenges and am open to the goodness that awaits me with each new chance.

By letting go of expecting ease or perfection, I allow myself to discover possibilities in every situation. I create my own happiness even in the midst of challenges.

**Self-reflection questions:**

Am I waiting for perfection to be happy?
Do I perceive challenges as obstacles or opportunities?
What unexpected opportunity for gratitude has slipped by me?

# Top 10 Ways Gratitude Can Enhance the Value of Your Life

Abundance surrounds you in many ways. Regardless of where you are in life, there are numerous things that bring you fulfillment. What are you grateful for right now? Take a moment to reflect on that.

Consider how gratitude can make your life better:

**You'll become more enthusiastic**

Research shows that individuals who regularly wrote down what they were grateful for in gratitude journals had higher levels of enthusiasm for life compared to those who didn't journal their gratitude. Embrace your gratitude. You'll be glad you did!

**You'll feel more determined to achieve your goals**

When you notice the good things, you're more likely to put your nose to the grindstone and work toward what you desire.

**Your level of optimism will increase**

According to several studies, those who documented what they were grateful for had a more positive outlook on how their lives were going and would unfold. Being an optimist fuels your passion for building the life you deserve.

**Energy levels will rise**

When you're grateful, you'll have more energy to create the life you desire. Being aware of what you're grateful for stimulates your efforts to uncover all that your life can be.

**You'll pay more attention**

Being grateful ensures that you're more attentive and aware of how your life is unfolding, what you're doing, and how you can further build the life you seek.

**You'll experience a decrease in stress levels**

Living in a state of gratitude diminishes the power of things that used to stress you out. Instead, you'll be deeply rooted in the wonderful world you inhabit.

**You'll find more joy in life**

Those who consciously experience gratitude decrease their chances of experiencing depression.

**You'll exercise more**

Those who express gratitude had more exercise reports than those who didn't keep gratitude journals.

**It'll be easier for you to provide help to others**

When you notice all the positive things around you, you'll be more in-clined to lend a helping hand. When your soul is filled with light and positivity, you'll feel a greater need to be present for others.

**You'll discover the life you truly desire**

Though it may sound remarkable, research on gratitude indicates that those who carry gratitude in their hearts are more likely to achieve their goals. As gratitude grows, your life dreams take shape.

Open your eyes to the rewards within your reach. As you do, you'll live a more fulfilling life. Allow yourself to feel the passion of autumn leaves, the serenity of falling snow, or the beauty of a clear blue sky. Notice the touch of warm hair on your skin or the love in a child's embrace. Perhaps you're even grateful for that first cup of morning coffee?

Start creating your own Chronicles of Gratitude Land today. Write about everything you're grateful for. As you begin to give thanks, your dreams will come true.

# I need time to reflect on my blessings

I am a blessed individual because I have more than I could ever imagine. The things I have, love, and enjoy the most are things I could never have provided for myself. That is why I am blessed.

Acknowledging that I am blessed is the key to living in a state of gratitude. Every day, I take the time to sit and think about the things I love most in the world. My family, my children, and even my material accomplishments are blessings.

I can't do anything to earn or deserve my blessings. Similarly, there is nothing I can do to make myself unworthy of them.

The beauty of blessings is that they are gifts given to me by my Creator out of love. Blessings are a way to reflect how deeply I am loved and how great my purpose is.

I am blessed even when my bank account is nearly empty or things aren't going well. Simply breathing the air is a gift. When I consider everything I have received as a blessing, I am filled with gratitude.

I do this to pause every day and look around. Wherever I am, whether at home or outside, there is so much beauty around me, even in mundane matters and experiences.

Today, I decided to take a step back and cultivate awareness of my blessings. I slow down to grasp the fragility of life and the gift I have. When I take the time to count my blessings, I experience true gratitude.

**Self-reflection questions:**

What am I grateful for today?
How can I refrain from taking many gifts for granted?
What does it mean to be blessed?

# I am grateful for the abundance I experience every day

I am filled with joy and gratitude for everything I have. I am blessed to have such a powerful abundance within myself and in my life.

Every day, I take the time to count my many blessings. I am fortunate to enjoy good health, wealth, and the pleasures of life. I deserve these things because I take daily action to nurture them. I make my health, finances, and happiness a priority.

My friends and family are a powerful source of abundance. I am both a recipient and a giver of great love, respect, and admiration. The people in my life constantly remind me of my value to the world. I am inherently important and precious.

Whatever I need, I experience it. All the resources I crave to live an exciting and fruitful life are around me. My greatest task is to identify the necessary resources, which is why I invite mindfulness and focus into my actions. Whatever I need, I will surely notice it quickly and easily. I know what I need and I know how to obtain it.

While I enjoy unlimited abundance, I avoid the burden of hoarding excessive possessions. I take what I need, but I remain free from greedy accumulation. Living this way allows me to maintain space and a clear mind.

Today, I give thanks for everything I have. The world's riches belong to me to enjoy and use when needed. I am grateful for the abundance I experience every day.

**Self-reflection questions:**

What fills me with a sense of gratitude and what power within me?
How can I be more open to abundance in my life?
What has hindered or blocked me from receiving abundance, and how?

# By incorporating affirmations into your gratitude practice, you bring peace into your life

What are you grateful for?

Starting the day with specific gratitude affirmations is a great way to remind yourself of all the wonderful things you have in your life. When you vocalize these gratitude affirmations, you energize yourself and gain the courage to face all the challenges and adventures that each moment or day may bring.

By acknowledging your gratitude, you help recognize that you can have what you desire and need to find satisfaction in every moment of your life. Joy, money, love, and happiness belong to you; you deserve them!

Affirmations are easy to create, and it doesn't take much time. Within a few minutes, you can turbocharge your day better than a rocket-powered cup of coffee. By focusing on your well-being and abundance, you will surpass your highest level!

## Gratitude Affirmations and Stress

When you invite affirmations into your mornings (you can recite them at any time during the day or night), you will notice that your inner world becomes significantly less stressed. As you subconsciously understand that you can have everything you need and desire, your stress will start to fade away. Your negative reactions will be quieted and released. Now, you can enjoy peace of mind and carefreeness like never before.

## Here are 12 highly effective affirmations:

1. I feel an abundance of gratitude for everything I have and receive every day.
2. My needs and desires are generously fulfilled. I am thankful for them.
3. I am grateful for the harmony in my body, the health, love, and goodness that life reveals to me.
4. I am constantly amazed at how abundant my life is! I am always thriving. My abundant blessings, as well as my challenges, make me

better, stronger, and more alive.
5. I am grateful for everything I experience in this life. I am feeling, discovering, and growing.
6. I am deeply grateful for every person and every thing in my life.
7. I appreciate everything I have and express sincere gratitude to my loved ones.
8. The universe pours joy into my life every day. My cup is overflowing with wealth, health, and love.
9. My life is unique, extraordinary, and wonderful. I am deeply grateful for it.
10. I clearly see the beauty of life blooming around me.
11. I express gratitude for the infinite treasures I perceive, both seen and unseen.
12. I am grateful for my blessed ancestors who live on through my blood.

Using the above statements along with your own will help you lead a less stressful and more fulfilling life. Spending time with positive affirmations, appreciating everything you have, and everything you intend to achieve is one of the easiest "stress remedies" you will ever take. Affirmations have no side effects and are free. Choose peace in your life by harnessing the power of affirmations and gratitude.

## Express Your Feelings in Peace with the Help of Gratitude

In his poem "A Poison Tree," the great poet William Blake wrote:

"I was angry with my friend: I told my wrath, my wrath did end. I was angry with my foe: I told it not, my wrath did grow."

When you suppress your feelings, both positive and negative, you hold yourself back from being all that you can be. Not only that, but if you internalize your emotions, you grow like the "poisonous tree" that William Blake wrote about.

**Don't sow the seeds of a poison tree.**

When you hide your true feelings, there is internal pressure that causes negative emotions such as anger, resentment, fear, and hatred to swell and take on more potential energy. The fruition of such actions always comes when emotions explode outward due to the pressure.

When that happens, you may say words you don't mean that can deeply hurt those you love the most. Potential negative actions and reactions stemming from suppressed feelings can fill the thickest notebooks, which is another reason to express your feelings in a peaceful manner!

By sincerely expressing your feelings, you can dispel negative energy and immediately start feeling a greater sense of peace within yourself. Eventually, you will feel less stress, tension, and anger when you release all your emotions. Constructively expressing your feelings will help you speak with greater sensitivity and perceive the good in others more rationally.

**Gratitude helps us navigate the path of self-expression.**

Now, openly expressing your negative feelings doesn't mean you should treat others harshly by dressing your anger in sinister words. It also doesn't mean pointing fingers or accusing others of what you feel. Instead, find a more constructive way to release what needs to be released. Perhaps it would be best to write down your feelings and send them in an email. If you have creative skills, write a poem or song about your emotions. Whatever you do, focus on the issue rather than the person. After all, we all make mistakes!

If you feel you can't be as deeply open about your feelings, always express gratitude. For example, you can start with a compliment and gradually express your frustrations. If you feel like you have nothing to be grateful for, you're not looking deep enough and firmly enough within yourself. There is plenty of joy in your life that can overpower your negative emotions. For instance, did you have a nutritious breakfast this morning? Then you have something to be grateful for! Have you ever had a satisfying conversation with a loved one that made you see a situation with fresh eyes? Then you have something to be grateful for!

Focus primarily on those positive, fulfilling experiences, and then express your feelings openly and honestly. With an attitude of gratitude for all that you have, you will feel confident in your right to express what you feel.

Why did Blake willingly share his anger with his friend? He cared about him and was grateful to have him, so he wanted to immediately dispel his anger. However, when it came to his foe, Blake wasn't as grateful and instead suffered greatly when the poisonous tree awakened in his soul.

Remember, your spirit resides within you and influences how you think, feel, and act. So seek peace in your heart and mind with the power of gratitude, awakening the energy of love within you!

# Elevate Your Mood to a Higher Level with These 6 Gratitude-Building Strategies

Most of us are constantly under pressure due to the fast pace of modern life. It's natural to feel tired or even a bit powerless from time to time.

The good news is that there's something as simple as focusing on the challenges and acknowledging the things you're grateful for in your life. It can immediately improve your mood.

Regular practice of gratitude can enhance your mood, as well as increase self-worth, willpower, long-term health, and even levels of success in life!

Overcome internal turmoil with these practices that will help you develop a sense of gratitude:

1. Make and keep a gratitude list. The next time you feel angry, frustrated, or a bit down, make a list and literally count your blessings. Creating a list helps you stop obsessively thinking about the current situation.

    *Don't limit yourself to just one list. Consider keeping a gratitude journal to record things and events in your life that you're grateful for. Over time, you'll create a tangible record of all the positive aspects of your life.

2. Start your day with positives. Set the right tone and sharpness for the rest of the day by taking a few moments each morning to focus on the positive things and experiences in your life.

    *Asking yourself questions can be a great way to focus on the positive aspects of your own life. Good questions to ask yourself include: "What good is happening right now?", "What possibilities await me today?", or "Am I grateful for love?".

3. Be mindful of the good around you. It's hard to maintain a positive attitude if you only focus on negative events around you. Make a conscious effort to seek out the good in everything, especially in small, simple things like a child's innocent laughter or the beauty found in na-

ture.

4. Perform random acts of kindness. You can increase your gratitude by being someone else's evidence of gratitude. Practice random acts of kindness by unexpectedly helping others.

*What may seem like a small act to you can be a significant act of generosity for someone in need. Seek opportunities every day to help someone else. The other person will be grateful for your generosity, and you will be grateful for the increase in self-worth and mood.

5. A picture is worth a thousand words. Why not document the things you're grateful for by taking pictures? You can even spread positive thoughts by sharing your gratitude photos on social media.

6. Collect gratitude notes as loose pieces in a jar. Are you too busy to make gratitude lists or keep a gratitude journal? Try writing short notes of gratitude to yourself and keep them in a jar!

*When you need encouraging words, reach for one of the notes and read it to instantly open up to a new possibility of perception!

*As the year comes to an end, look back at the gratitude notes to remind yourself of all the good things that happened during it. Also, focus on shorter time frames and track your progress on a timeline, describing the moment of entry into the process and the accompanying states at each here and now, and the ongoing reference point will show you the progress you've made.

Every person faces difficult times in life, but regularly practicing gratitude gives you the power and inspiration to stay positive as you overcome challenges. It will be the drums that wake you up to fight. Just listen to your depth right now, do you hear their sound?

# I can always find something to be grateful for

I welcome the small gifts that life presents me with every day. I appreciate the beauty that surrounds me in nature and people.

I am fortunate to live in a place that allows for the cultivation of beautiful flowers. I cherish their natural fragrance.

I am grateful for the kindness I receive when I encounter a stranger. I realize that I am lucky to have the privilege of meeting people who are kind for no reason.

I strive to maintain an open and positive mindset. With an open mind, I can clearly see the blessings in my everyday life. A positive mind can transform most disappointments into life lessons that will positively impact my future.

By releasing what needs to be released.

I am grateful for what I have because I know that there are others who have much less than me. I am aware that there are others who are struggling to survive.

Today, I acknowledge that gratitude for the life I have rewards my soul with contentment and happiness. I am grateful for all the wonderful people and things in my life.

**Self-reflection questions:**

What am I most grateful for today?
What small gifts did I notice today?
How can I show appreciation for my blessings?

# 13 ways to say "Thank you"

One of the most powerful phrases in any language is the word "thank you."

With this word, you can express appreciation for a kind gesture or favor someone has done for you. This word holds great power in its deep nature. To explore more possibilities for expressing gratitude, try one of these 13 ways to say "thank you."

To uncover the possibilities within you, try my suggestions:

1. Smile. Express your gratitude with a smile, and the other person will almost always smile back. If they are having a bad day, your smile may be the initiating factor that changes their day.

2. Send a note. If you're shy, you may find it easier to express yourself through writing. If writing intimidates you, simply write a short note expressing your gratitude. Your heartfelt words will mean more to the recipient than the most beautiful prose or poetry. You can start by sending yourself a text message or writing through Messenger.

3. Buy a special gift. Look for a small item that you can give as a token of appreciation. If you have concerns about the positive effect of your actions, try buying coffee or sending chocolates. You can also ask your friends for ideas.

4. Invite friends, or maybe strangers. Say "thank you" by spending time together. Do something that will bring them joy.

5. Share your story. Brag to others about what someone has done for you. They will likely hear how valuable you speak of them. Even better—brag about them in front of them. This will enhance their reputation and self-confidence at the same time.

6. Offer a favor. Let the person choose what favor you can do for them. A small favor often helps someone in a big way.

7. Buy a ticket to an event. Find a local concert or show that brings po-

sitive impressions and emotions.

8. Contribute to charity. Learn about what your friends are passionate about, then make a donation to the appropriate charitable organization on their behalf.

9. Add a personal touch to everything you create. Say "thank you" for every little thing and show it through every gift. The person will recognize your intention and appreciate the gesture. You can make a handmade card or create a slideshow. Create something sentimental that truly expresses your appreciation.

10. Phone call. Sometimes a simple phone call is enough to deliver the message. In addition to the phone call to say "thank you," regularly call and check on how they're doing. Offer your friendship.

11. Give a "gift of the month." For someone who always does nice things for you, consider a gift in the form of a subscription to their favorite magazine. You can also prepay for a subscription to a "book of the month" club that covers topics they find interesting.

12. Give a gift card. If you're having trouble finding the perfect gratitude gift, consider a gift card from a local shopping center or online store that sells various products. This way, your loved ones will definitely receive something they like.

13. Bake something at home. If you enjoy baking, your talents can be a sweet way to show gratitude. Everyone appreciates delicious homemade desserts.

The only limit to everything that can happen is your imagination. If you go the extra mile to show someone that you are truly grateful, that gesture will be remembered for a long time. Significantly strengthen relationships in your life. Choose one of these ideas or come up with your own and say "thank you" to someone special in a meaningful way.

# I am full of gratitude, and I have an abundance of it

All my needs and many of my desires are being met. People who care about me surround me, showering me with their love, and I am aware of their love. For this reason, I am full of gratitude.

So many people in the world are not having their basic needs met: food, shelter, clean water. Many are simply struggling to survive each day. When I think about these things, I remember how truly blessed I am. Regardless of what the future may bring, today I have food, shelter, clean water, and these gifts are deserving of my gratitude.

Every day, I take a few moments to remind myself of my blessings. I think about the people who love me. I spend a moment mentally sending love and gratitude to all of them.

I remember and acknowledge the ways in which problems are being solved, which is why life is easy for me. I have gifts and talents to share. Many things come easily to me, even if my life is challenging. Other things may come harder, but I know that they are all opportunities for learning.

I intentionally cultivate gratitude even in difficult life situations.

If I ever feel that my gratitude is dwindling and counting my blessings doesn't seem to help, I take a moment to step off that path and do something good for someone else. By helping others, I remind myself that the world is an abundant place. And when I remember that, I am grateful.

Today, I am grateful for the blessings in my life. I need to take the time to be aware of each one. With all the abundance surrounding me, I am full of gratitude.

**Self-reflection questions:**

What can I be grateful for today?
How can I serve someone today?
In what ways does being helpful to others increase my gratitude?

## 5 Benefits of Gratitude

Expressing gratitude can be a great way to spread positive feelings in the world around us. When you think about it, achieving your goals starts with a positive thought.

How do you feel when someone sincerely expresses gratitude for something you've done? Doesn't it make you feel good about yourself? Such positive emotions give us strength, enhance our enthusiasm, and motivate us to achieve even more.

Feeling grateful for what you have can generate good feelings and sustain patience in pursuing goals.
This shows that practicing gratitude effectively can have a snowball effect.

Here are some benefits of gratitude:

1. Goal achievement. When you feel gratitude, it is a lasting and selfless feeling. It is much more than just a temporary surge of positive energy. It has the power to ground and imprint itself in our energetic fields, providing a great boost to positive vibrations.
    *When expressing your gratitude to others, make sure you are open and clear. People don't know what you're thinking. By verbalizing it, you can change that.

2. Strengthened relationships. There are many ways to express gratitude to your loved ones, including saying "thank you," writing a letter, or giving them a thoughtful gift. When you learn to avoid taking your loved ones for granted, you will have a long-lasting and loving relationship.
    *Gratitude is a two-way street. Learn how to effectively express your gratitude and, equally important, how to receive it.

3. Improved communication. Gratitude can mean better communication among beings. By expressing your gratitude to strangers, you are more likely to initiate the same process in them.
    *Gratitude is such a powerful unit that it can even help you com-

municate with animals! It is something to be appreciated.

4. More effective constructive criticism. No matter how we express constructive criticism, it often makes the recipient defensive or even angry. No one likes a blow to their ego. In this situation, invoking a grateful attitude may take a while. You can effectively deliver criticism by emphasizing what you appreciate, using the contrast of good and bad.

5. Preserving memories. You can preserve memories in a positive way when you keep a Chronicles of Gratitude. You will be able to relive those memories again when reading about those happy times and moments from the past.

*Express your gratitude every day. Expressing gratitude to others may seem like a selfless act, but it is also something to benefit from. When you express your gratitude every day, you change your way of thinking.

Keep in mind that appreciating your good life occurs when most of your thoughts remain positive. Negative thoughts can sometimes be overwhelming, but just because you have them doesn't mean you are a bad person. They come to everyone, but you can strive to minimize them through a grateful attitude.

One way to express your gratitude every day is to remind yourself of the grand, positive picture of our higher purpose of being when negative thoughts arise. If a small argument with your spouse makes you feel angry and resentful, take a deep breath and pause for a moment, shifting your point of reference. Remember that arguments are not permanent, and instead, feel gratitude for the gift of that relationship. Everything passes, good and bad, it is a symbolism clothed in the possibility of experiencing, it's the menu card in the most expensive restaurant of your feast called life.

Our days on this Earth are numbered, so we must cherish the time we have and enjoy the blessings of life every day as if they were our last moments.

# Every action I take has roots in gratitude

My daily actions are intentional. I choose to go through life with a grateful mindset. This focus allows me to maintain a positive life.
When I arrive at work every day, I remind myself that having a job is a luxury. Being grateful for employment motivates me to work diligently.

Before greeting a friend or a stranger, I express gratitude for the opportunity to see them and engage in conversation. My initial impressions set a positive tone for our interaction.

The simple blessings of life are apparent to me with every step I take. I move purposefully and enthusiastically because I am blessed with the ability to walk. I avoid mind-wandering and immerse myself in the present moment, even when I feel down. Gratitude guides my steps.

Maintaining calmness when disciplining my children can be challenging at times. However, my children are precious gifts who deserve proper guidance. I use this reminder to keep my mission clear when imparting life lessons to them. When they know how much of a blessing they are to me, my work is done well.

Today, gratitude is a natural part of my life. I celebrate the opportunity to showcase my grateful mindset. Recognizing goodness in life allows me to live happily and peacefully.

**Self-reflection questions:**

What things or moments am I most grateful for?
How can I use my positive thinking to counteract negative energy from others?
In what situations do I find it challenging to focus on being grateful?

# I appreciate the beauty that flows from the gifts of nature

When I step outside each day, I look around, inhale the air, and feel the wind on my face. The beauty of the natural environment strikes me, and I feel surrounded by the arms of nature. Today may be my best or worst day, but regardless, nature is there, outside, waiting to guide me through my life.

I feel grateful every time I think about the world of nature. Even though I believe it will always be there for me, I still hungrily breathe in its pure joy when I see deep purple flowers on bushes or snowflakes falling from the sky. The lush, green grass flying tickles my nose with its aroma and urges me to stay outside a few more minutes.

When a troubling thought haunts me, I take a walk in the fresh air. I breathe in and out, and the scents of nature and caresses of the wind come to meet me. Every time, I find what I need to carry on with my day.

When I am face-to-face with nature, I momentarily forget about what has been happening so far. Any unsettling feelings I experienced dissolve, and I am sustained by nature's sweet song.

Today, I promise to closely observe the backdrop of nature—the color of the sky, its delicate scent in the air, and the sound of whispering trees calling out to me. The pervasive beauty of nature uplifts my spirits.

**Self-reflection questions:**

Are there moments when I yearn to see everything nature provides?
Do I seize every opportunity to rest in the embrace of nature?
Regardless of my mood on any given day, how can I utilize opportunities to turn to nature for comfort and support for my soul?

# I am grateful for everything I have

When I reflect on everything I possess, I realize that my wealth is abundant. Sometimes I wonder what image and colors my happiness has. From my home to my work, my life is filled with many things that bring me joy, intrigue, and sustenance.

I live in a comfortable home that entices me with its charms after a hard day's work. Everything and everyone I love seems to welcome me as I walk through the door. I am immediately rejuvenated when I reach my humble abode.

My life is overflowing with wealth beyond measure because of the beautiful people I have in my life.

My loved ones accept my strengths and weaknesses. My partner understands me, and my relatives are helpful and supportive when I need them. My friends are within reach to celebrate my successes, motivate me, and support my endeavors.

My work supports and strengthens my actions. The projects I work on ignite my interest. I am so happy that I get paid for doing what I love. When it comes to my work, I ask for broader opportunities to experience it.

Today, I am making a list of the people, places, and things I am grateful for. It is important to acknowledge everything I have in this life. I am grateful for my wealth.

**Self-reflection questions:**

How often do I reflect on everything I have in my life?
Why is it important to express my gratitude?
When have I struggled to notice what I am grateful for?

# Show your gratitude, dressed in compliments, to others

Do you enjoy receiving compliments? They are great for boosting our self-worth, and everyone feels good hearing words that show respect or admiration as added value. Those few words lift our spirits and give us wings.

Compliments confirm that we are doing something well and that our efforts are appreciated. It only takes a moment to notice something small about someone, but those few words can certainly impact their day.

**Value your family.**

Expressing gratitude to those you love serves a dual purpose: it shows how grateful you are for their presence in your life and also acknowledges the special work they do.

Here are a few examples of expressing gratitude:

"Thank you for doing the dishes. You did a great job!"

"I truly appreciate your help with dinner tonight. It was a fantastic meal."

"I am so grateful for your love and support. You really helped me get through a tough day."

This encourages both children and adults to be more helpful. When praised and given positive recognition, it sticks with them longer. Regularly hearing compliments also teaches children how to appreciate people in their lives.

**Honor your coworkers.**

In business, there are two types of managers: those who appreciate their employees for a job well done and those who expect work to be done without any motivation or acknowledgment from their side. Of course, we all need to treat each other with the respect and dignity we deserve!

What kind of manager are you?

Here are a few examples of expressing gratitude in the workplace:

"Thank you for your efficient work today. I will let the boss know how hard you've been working lately."

"The client loved the report you wrote." "I really appreciate you taking the time to help me. It means a lot to me!"

Compliments given in the office can be a huge motivator for our employees. Your colleagues will trust and respect you much more than anyone else in the office.

**Compliment strangers.**

In today's society, very few people take the time to strike up a conversation with strangers. We must remember that people come into our lives for various reasons, and you can deeply affect someone's mood simply by being kind to them.

Of course, you probably shouldn't disclose your entire life story the first time you meet someone, but you can say something nice about the person you come in contact with. Show your gratitude for encountering that person because that experience may teach you something new about yourself.

Here are a few examples based on which you can seek opportunities to give someone a sincere compliment:

•Is the person cheerful?
•Is the person genuinely kind to others?
•Are this person's children very well-behaved?
•Have you seen this person do something kind for someone else?

The key to expressing gratitude is to open your eyes to the simple gifts throughout the day. By paying attention to the actions of those around you, you not only help others gain confidence, but you also become known as a trustworthy man or woman.

Make an effort to praise at least one person each day. You will begin to appreciate the little things in life and brighten someone's day in the process.

# The more grateful I am, the more reasons I find to be grateful

Being grateful comes easily to me, and I find reasons to be grateful every day.

When I wake up in the morning, I mentally list the things I am grateful for in my life. Every time I face a challenge, I remind myself of the many blessings I have. Being grateful makes my life richer and easier.

Being grateful for the little things in life is an extraordinary way to live. I appreciate the small things, and I believe that the more grateful I am, the more reasons I stimulate to create new layers of gratitude.

Being grateful is not always easy, but if I find myself in a difficult situation, I intentionally seek something positive in it. I can always find something good. Now I can smile in any situation and realize that it is a gift.

When I go to bed, I reflect again on what I am grateful for. This simple habit always brings me joy and fills me with hope. My life is so wonderful.

I am blessed, and my blessings are too numerous to even count. I am the happiest person in the world. I constantly receive good things in life. I appreciate everything I have and wish for everyone to be as happy as I am.

Today, I look at my life with gratitude. In every situation, I find the positive. I see perfection in every person, and I feel that the world is good. The more grateful I am, the more things I notice to be grateful for.

**Self-reflection questions:**

What am I grateful for in my life?
What could I be grateful for?
How would I benefit from a stronger sense of gratitude?
How can I experience and cultivate a more "juicy" gratitude?

# Some of my greatest blessings are invisible

Houses and cars are useful, but some of my greatest blessings are invisible. Every day, I take time to recognize both internal and external blessings.

My health is invaluable. Being fit and strong allows me to provide for my family and explore the world. I make choices that help me lead a long and active life. This includes plenty of rest, exercise, and green vegetables.

My peace of mind is equally priceless. I desire the happiness and satisfaction that comes from knowing I am loved.

The quality of my life also has a spiritual dimension. I engage in practices that are meaningful to me. I surround myself with people who provide guidance and encouragement for meaningful experiences and physical and spiritual growth.

My eyes show me many wonderful things, and I count on my ears, nose, and fingers to provide me with experiences as well. I pay attention to beautiful sounds, scents, and textures. I listen to the songs of birds and the ringing of church bells. I feel the flowers and freshly cut grass. I dip my hand in cool water.

I focus on my breath to turn my attention inward. I sit to meditate or pause during my daily activities. I explore the causes of my emotions and express gratitude for them.

To connect with the world around me, I slow down. I close my eyes and allow the smile of my inner child, along with a favorite symphony, to fill my mind and body.

Today, I focus on the blessings I may not have noticed until now. My heart is filled with gratitude and joy.

**Self-reflection questions:**

How do my material possessions positively impact the lives of others?
What intangible elements make my life better?
How can I become more grateful for all my blessings?

# My blessings are countless

Every day, I receive countless blessings. When I pause to contemplate the significant aspects of my life, I am in awe. My list of accomplishments far outweighs any negative events in my life.

Having basic skills is a blessing that many take for granted. My healthy body and mind allow me to achieve great things every day. I fully utilize my time and am grateful for fulfilling my daily tasks and achieving set goals.

My hard work results in recognition from my employer. My efforts lead to success, which I consider a blessing.

Whenever I feel the urge to complain or express disappointment, I remind myself that I am a magnificent being striving for excellence. By making an effort, I pause and reflect on all the benefits of life that I experience.

I find blessings in the most unexpected places. When I look into the eyes of a hungry child, I am grateful for the opportunity to offer them a meal.

The opportunity to help someone is a blessing in itself. It is an exercise in humility that helps me appreciate where I am now. I embrace learning from new life lessons.

Today, I am excited about all the blessings I experience each day. I embrace finding goodness in every situation. I continue to express gratitude for all the choices life presents me on my path.

**Self-reflection questions:**

How can I improve my behavior when I feel like complaining?
What inspires me to make positive changes in my life?
How can I transform a negative situation into a positive one?

# CHAPTER 12



## V is elixir is for you

The power of gratitude radically transforms the lives of millions of people, and it is a wonderful solution that can be quickly learned. When you start to recognize the force of energy that is around us and within us, you will begin to express gratitude for everything you perceive and receive, awakening even greater happiness and profound satisfaction with your life. Gratitude will awaken in you the need for focus, infuse you with the nectar of hope for the future, and awaken in you the magical power of reciprocation here and now.

Start practicing the attitude of gratitude, breathe new life and experiences into yourself, making such a powerful act as gratitude an integral part of each day, awakening mental, physical, and psychological benefits.

Thank you for the time spent together :) - Gregory Jaszewski

You can contact me through my website: http://grzegorzjaszewski.eu/
See you soon.

# GOOD TO KNOW

## Achieve access to the cosmic wisdom of the universe and create miracles in your life.

The Akashic Records are an infinite source of knowledge, containing every thought and action that has ever taken place in the universe. It is said to be a field of information stored on a non-physical plane of existence, accessible to those who know how to access it.

The Akashic Records hold a vast wealth of ancient knowledge and memories that have been stored in this mystical realm for thousands of years. This collective universal consciousness contains all the information about each soul's journey through time, including past incarnations and experiences. Access to the Akashic Records is available to anyone who has an open heart, a clear mind, and a sincere commitment to spiritual growth and delving deep into their own consciousness.

As you enter the energetic Kingdom of the Akashic Records, take a few moments to connect with yourself and become aware of the present moment. Imagine any energies that may disrupt this process gently dissipating, allowing you to be fully open to receiving whatever is meant to be revealed. Open your heart and mind and trust that only information meant for your highest good will be unveiled.

Visualize a surrounding field of pure white light enveloping you, filling you with divine love and protection. With each breath, allow yourself to release any fear or doubt you may have, trusting that everything will unfold exactly as it should. Kindly ask the guardians of the Akashic Records to support you in accessing the Records, ensuring that everything comes to light in a way that serves your highest recognition. If needed, you can always ask for guidance during this journey by posing questions to yourself.

When we gain access to the Akashic Records, we are privileged to tap into the divine truth of our existence. In doing so, we can transform our lives and manifest dreams that once seemed out of reach.

The Akashic Records are a powerful tool for those seeking to uncover the mysteries of the universe and master the art of creating their own reality.

When you feel ready, express gratitude to the guardians of the Akashic Records for their wisdom and presence. Offer gratitude for everything they have prepared for you, knowing that they will always hear your inquiries. Finally, the time has come to open the Book of Life—the Akashic Records—and discover ancient secrets.

Connecting with the Akashic Records helps us remember who we truly are and why we are here. As we learn to access its power, we discover our true selves and uncover our purpose on this earth. Through the Akashic Records, we have the power to create lasting positive change in our personal and collective lives. The Akashic Records are also known as the Fifth Element or the Information Field, and the key to their gates lies within you, so travel freely and enjoy their energy.

# ABOUT GREGORY

Grzegorz Jaszewski is an entrepreneur residing in the United Kingdom who loves sharing knowledge and helping others in self-discovery. Grzegorz Jaszewski is a person who practices exploring the world and oneself. He has discovered a key that can open secret doors for you as well: the only constant in life is change—if you don't step onto its path yourself, you will be changed by someone else.

x e message of Grzegorz Jaszewski can be summarized in a few words: "I believe that knowledge is power, and everyone should strive to improve themselves and/or their business, regardless of the stage of life they are in; whether it's to enhance their mind or increase profits."

**Bibliography:**


Algoe, S.B., Haidt, J., Gable, S.L. (2008). Beyond reciprocity: Gratitude and relationships in everyday life. Emotion, 8(3), 425-429.

Bartlett, M.Y., DeSteno, D. (2006). Gratitude and prosocial behavior helping when it costs you. Psychological Science, 17(4), 319-325.

Bretz, S.L., McClary, L. (2014). Students' understandings of acid strength: How meaningful is reliability when measuring alternative conceptions? Journal of Chemical Education, 92(2), 212-219.


Above, I have presented the first three positions from a large number of books that I used while writing "Codes of Gratitude." You can find the full list under the following link:

https://docs.google.com/document/d/13DIrv3SUZ_y5Hmb_
WDEUGhR6JHAz7uPuq0TQKm30dw0/edit?usp=sharing

*Keep in mind that the quotes int this book have been translated by a translator, so they are not in their original form.*

www.ingramcontent.com/pod-product-compliance
Lightning Source LLC
Chambersburg PA
CBHW071212130726
47998CB00002B/711